ALL-AMERICA ROSES

by rayford clayton reddell

photographs by saxon holt

CHRONICLE BOOKS

SAN FRANCISCO

This book is dedicated to Dan Bifano, an All-America rosarian.

Text copyright © 1998 by Rayford Clayton Reddell
Photographs copyright © 1998 by Saxon Holt

Library of Congress Cataloging-in-Publication Data.
Reddell, Rayford Clayton.
All-America roses / by Rayford Clayton Reddell; photographs by Saxon Holt.
p. cm. Includes index. ISBN 0-8118-1845-4 (hardcover)
1. Roses—Varieties. 2. Roses—Varieties—Pictorial works.
3. Roses—Awards—United States. 4. All-America Rose Selections, Inc.
I. Holt, Saxon. II. Title. SB411.6.R44 1998 635.9'33734—dc21 97-30400 CIP

Printed in Hong Kong

Cover and book design by Gregory Design, San Francisco

The photographer wishes to thank Ann Leyhe for scouting and styling assistance.
Thanks to those gardeners who grew the roses: Garden Valley Ranch, Phyllis Saccani,
John Dallas, Filoli Gardens, Katie Trefethen, Sonoma Mission Garden, John Traulson,
Sally Robertson, Carol Grant, Mrs. Vella, Richard Cunningham, Patrick Cearley.

Distributed in Canada by Raincoast Books
8680 Cambie Street
Vancouver, B.C. V6P 6M9

10   9   8   7   6   5   4   3   2   1

Chronicle Books
85 Second Street
San Francisco, CA 94105
Web Site: www.chronbooks.com

TABLE OF CONTENTS

INTRODUCTION

During the first years I grew roses seriously, I was an outspoken critic of All-America roses. Many of the crowned varieties were no more than ordinary in my own garden, while others had proved to be such losers that they weren't even in commerce anymore.

Making such allegations in writing proved costly. When I said that I had never even seen 'Jiminy Cricket', a winner from 1955, a reader wrote to me and told me in no uncertain terms that 'Jiminy Cricket' was her grandmother's favorite rose and hers, too, and that I should keep such caustic comments to myself.

Another reader wrote that 'Oregold' was the yellowest rose he knew—how could I not like it? Still, I wondered why certain stinkers had walked away with the prize. I decided to find out by becoming an official judge.

all-america rose selections, incorporated

All-America Rose Selections, Incorporated, a nonprofit research corporation, was founded in 1938 for the purpose of evaluating new rose varieties thought to be potentially worthy of a special stamp of approval. As stated in their bylaws, the specific purposes of AARS are:

"(a) To foster the development, production, and distribution of new and better roses in and for the United States of America.

"(b) To foster the establishment and maintenance of rose Test and Demonstration Gardens in the United States of America, for the purpose of testing, judging, rating, and demonstrating new and undisseminated kinds, species, and varieties, and acquainting the people with the most worthy roses and their uses.

"(c) To make awards to new rose varieties of superior quality and marked distinction as determined by their performance in the All-America Rose official Test Gardens and to publicize and recommend those varieties which receive such awards."

In order to make certain that winning roses perform well across the country, official test gardens are selected with an eye toward their specific location. Presently there are 22 test sites. Their locations and official judges are listed in Appendix A.

Official test gardens are open to the public (a contingency for qualification), so you can look for yourself at roses headed down the pike. Don't visit expecting to learn names of what takes your fancy, though. Test roses are identified by a 6-digit number and don't get named until they're introduced into commerce. Take notes on numbered roses that appeal to you, however, planning to ask later if they either won or will be named and sold anyway.

Currently, six types of roses are eligible as entries: Hybrid Teas, Floribundas, Grandifloras, Miniatures, Climbers, and, since 1985, Landscape roses. Official gardens are supplied with four plants of each entry (the entries need not have originated in the United States as long as they have never been offered for sale here).

Officiating judges are instructed to "give roses under test commonsense care," including planting in good soil; regular spraying, feeding, and irrigation; judicious pruning; and, where necessary, winter protection. Scores for entries are due no later than July 1 and November 1 each year for two years of trial (Climbing roses are judged for three years). Scoring on official sheets, judges mark entries on a 5-point scale (poor to excellent) for these 15 attributes:

Novelty—Is the entry unique or too similar to roses already in commerce?

Form, buds—How pleasing is the petal assembly from tight bud to half-open blossoms?

Form, flowers—How appealing is the petal arrangement of blossoms from their half-open to fully open stages?

Color, buds—How attractive is the color of petals from tight bud to half-open blossoms?

Color, open blooms—How pretty is the color of flowers from their half-open to fully open stages?

Aging Quality—How well do flowers hold up as they mature? Does color remain pleasing?

Flowering Effect—What impact does the plant make when it's in full bloom? Are flowers well sized and proportioned?

Fragrance—Are flowers perfumed at any stage of their development? Can the aroma be described?

Stem/Cluster—Are stems strong enough to hold blooms upright? Are flowers held in harmonious balance to each other and the plant from which they grow?

Plant Habit—Considering height, girth, and general shape, how satisfactory is growth structure?

Vigor—Is growth continuous and robust?

Foliage—Are leaves abundant, well sized, and shapely?

Disease Resistance—Is the entry resistant to mildew, rust, and blackspot?

Repeat Bloom—Does the entry repeat its bloom with satisfactory regularity?

Personal Opinion—Overall, what do you think of the entry? Would you plant it in your own garden?

Following each judging session, scores are tabulated and forwarded to the AARS executive director, who holds a secret-ballot meeting of the test-garden voting members each winter. After two years of scoring, winners are selected, but they're not announced until the following year so that growers have time to bud extra plants of a surefire commercial success.

measuring up

Before becoming an official garden, test sites are first categorized as demonstration gardens, during which time all rules for official gardens apply, including scoring by the first of each July and November. Although the scores from demonstration-garden judges don't count in the final ballots that determine winners, they're benchmarks for assuring that prospective official judges can tell the difference between great, good, and so-so roses.

The first time I judged the roses in my demonstration garden, I fretted for weeks over the scores I gave them. When results from all gardens were tabulated, I was shocked to learn that the varieties I had selected best were considered no more than mediocre by official judges.

When I asked a long-timer in the system what was wrong, she suggested that my personal biases might be skewing my scores. I realized that she was right, that the rose varieties leading the trials were orange and red—not my favorite colors, especially if they're not fragrant. My vision of their overall qualities had been blinded by their color. I had to learn to keep personal opinion to myself (except for scoring that specific category, of course).

By the end of my second year as a demonstration judge, I began marching in step with the big guys and winners were almost always in my top-three list of roses in that particular category. I even began predicting winners after I had grown them for only one year. For instance, I knew that 'Carefree Delight', 'Scentimental', and 'Fame!' (selections in, respectively, 1996, 1997, and 1998) were big time when I first saw them bloom. Honesty compels me to admit that it didn't take a particularly well trained eye to spot these three winners; they all but grew with blue ribbons draped around them.

Still, I made some enemies whose lovingly created entries performed so well where they and several other test gardens grew them. My reply to such admonition has always been that I garden in Petaluma, California, and score test roses just as I see them perform here.

When you consider that the current 22 official test-garden sites offer complete climatic samplings, it's no surprise that I've made enemies; the reason is inherent to the All-America Selections system. What shines in Portland, Maine, may only piddle around in Portland, Oregon, and vice versa. Roses are often matters of local talent, and the goal of the AARS system is to find roses that perform so well that they transcend locale.

Except for 1951, when no selection was made, from 1940 through 1998, 163 roses have been declared All-America Selections.

The following is my personal selection of 40 varieties I believe have insured immortality, either owing to their exemplary performance or purely because of their sheer beauty. A complete list of winners is found in Appendix B (page 92).

'All That Jazz'	'Honor'
'Amber Queen'	'Intrigue'
'Angel Face'	'Medallion'
'Apricot Nectar'	'Mister Lincoln'
'Bewitched'	'Olympiad'
'Bonica'	'Paradise'
'Brandy'	'Pascali'
'Brass Band'	'Peace'
'Brigadoon'	'Perfect Moment'
'Carefree Delight'	'Queen Elizabeth'
'Cathedral'	'Royal Highness'
'Color Magic'	'Saratoga'
'Double Delight'	'Scentimental'
'Duet'	'Sheer Bliss'
'Europeana'	'Sheer Elegance'
'Fame!'	'Singin' in the Rain'
'First Prize'	'Tiffany'
'French Lace'	'Touch of Class'
'Golden Showers'	'Tournament of Roses'
'Granada'	'White Lightnin''

In 1987 'Bonica' won an All-America award in a brand-new category, Landscape roses. Gardeners went crazy; wanted, demanded more. Five years later, America's hybridizer Bill Twomey gave them some of what they wanted—'All That Jazz'.

Not a rose for the meek or small of garden, 'All That Jazz' is a hefty lass; a tall one, too. Bushes eagerly tower over 5 feet and, as they mature, insist on becoming rotund. Keep in mind, however, that such are the attributes of many good Landscape roses; that's where they're supposed to strut their stuff—in the landscape.

Many of the best attributes of 'All That Jazz' are reminiscent of old-fashioned garden roses; not just its bushy habit but also its flower form, with blooms that offer 9–12 frilly petals each.

'All That Jazz' knows no shame where color is concerned. Petals ranging in color from bright salmon to hot coral are surrounded by dense clusters of lemon yellow stamens. When it's in full bloom, and I do mean full, you'll literally blink in wonder at the flashy color combination (it may not be for you, but you must admit it's dazzling).

Foliage is deep green and glossy.

Of all the attributes gardeners demand in a Landscape rose, foremost is disease resistance. 'All That Jazz' has no time for disease, none whatsoever. Not only is it impervious to disease, 'All That Jazz' is bothered by neither heat nor cold. I think it could grow wild.

A M B E R Q U E E N

England's talented hybridizer Jack Harkness has introduced some exquisite roses to the world. In 1988 he graced rosedom with the Floribunda 'Amber Queen' and won an All-America award for the lovely effort.

If you plan on exhibiting roses, other varieties will bring you more ribbons. If you want to enjoy roses indoors, however (or simply harbor an abundance in the landscape), 'Amber Queen' is a must-have.

Heavily petaled for a Floribunda, 'Amber Queen' produces blossoms of 40 petals each. Plump in bud, the blooms mature large and cuppy. Whatever their ultimate form, the blossoms are miraculously colored shades of amber-yellow and almost always arrange themselves in sprays of three to five flowers each. In keeping with other similarly colored roses, 'Amber Queen' is deliciously fragrant. Foliage is handsome, too—large, copper-red to midgreen, and semiglossy. It's also abundant.

Perhaps this rose's finest contribution of all is inherent to its bushes—they prefer growing low to the ground and remaining the same size as each other. Such even-tempered habits not only make 'Amber Queen' a natural for use in borders and hedges, they help make her an ideal container rose.

ANGEL FACE

When America's Gladys Fisher hybridized 'Sterling Silver' for introduction in 1957, she became one of rosedom's most important benefactresses since Empress Josephine by offering mauve as a color for modern roses. Since then, the mauve color class has progressed to the point that its modern parent 'Sterling Silver' is no longer considered a strong contender for a mauve rose. The American Rose Society now rates it at 4.1 (lower than 6.0 is deemed "of questionable value"). I'd rate it even lower for its pitiful performance, and I dug up all of mine some years ago. Although people still ask for it, I believe this is mainly because they remember its rather catchy name and sumptuous fragrance. They don't know that some of the grandchildren of 'Sterling Silver' have even finer fragrance and growth habits far superior to that of their predecessor. Foremost is 'Angel Face', hybridized by southern California's Swim and Weeks in 1968 and an All-America Rose Selection for 1969—the first mauve rose to earn this prestigious award.

Buds are lovely and high centered. They open into 4-inch flat blooms with wavy petals around a center of golden stamens. Blooms keep well, even fully opened. 'Angel Face' has irresistible displays of typical Floribunda virtuosity: multiple blooms on one stem, often in all stages of development. Although others grow large bushes of 'Angel Face', mine are small. I believe that the fact that I cut almost every bloom that appears is surely a factor. I bet you might, too—that fragrance!

A P R I C O T   N E C T A R

Aptly named because of its delicious fruity fragrance, 'Apricot Nectar' was an All-America Selection in 1966. Besides its notorious fragrance, this winning Floribunda has several other fine qualities going for it.

First, the plant on which blossoms appear is vigorous, bushy, and well shaped.

Second, foliage is attractive, too. Not only is it abundant, it's emerald green, glossy, and resistant to disease.

Finally, and best of all, the blossoms. Formed in comely sprays at the end of each stem, buds start life with an ovoid shape but mature into fully double, cupped, large (up to 5 inches across) flowers. The basic bloom color is pinky apricot, but each petal boasts a golden base that literally glows.

Yet another winner from the hands of hybridizer Gene Boerner, 'Apricot Nectar' is also praised for the contribution it makes to the landscape. Unlike many modern hybrids, this rose doesn't grow rigidly upright. Instead, it chooses to present its bounty on arching, graceful bushes. Because of this natural growth habit, 'Apricot Nectar' makes a fine hedge rose, especially when cultivated next to a fence that can lend support in propping up the weighty sprays that appear all season long.

BEWITCHED

When people turn to me for advice on which pink rose they should grow, I make certain that they truly want pink, not a blend. If they do, 'Bewitched' is second to none.

One of the reasons 'Bewitched' won an All-America award for America's Walter Lammerts in 1967 is the purity of its color, the same reason it's so popular today. 'Bewitched' is fresh pink throughout, and the form of the bloom is lovely even when the blossoms are exceptionally large, as they're prone to be. 'Bewitched' is intensely fragrant, and its foliage is glossy olive green and of average disease resistance. Bushes are nicely shaped, upright, and vigorous.

'Bewitched' currently has a rating of only 7.3 by the American Rose Society. Don't let that put you off, however, because the reason why the rating is so low is of legitimate concern only to those who intend to exhibit their roses and realize that judges like perfectly straight stems. 'Bewitched' has what rosarians call a "crooked neck"—the stem just below the bloom is often shaped like a swan's neck. But don't confuse crooked necks with weak necks; the latter means that stems aren't strong enough to hold blooms erect. Crooked necks aren't necessarily weak, and no rose proves the point more resolutely than 'Bewitched', which holds its lovely blossoms tall, even when stems just below the blooms are shaped like an S curve.

Voting members of the American Rose Society should reconsider their rating of 'Bewitched'; it's a misleading assessment of one of the finest pink roses ever.

BONICA

'Bonica' is a landmark rose, and not only because it won an All-America award in 1987. More important, it did so in the newly created class of Landscape roses—varieties famed for their contribution to the landscape at large, rather than for perfection of bloom. Simultaneously, it set a standard for the new class of roses eligible for All-America status.

I didn't take well to 'Bonica' when I first saw it bloom, purely for personal, greedy reasons—I didn't see any commercial success from the sale of its blossoms that were, first, too loose and, second, on arching (rather than conventional, straight) stems. I wouldn't be able to sell them to my carriage floral trade.

Still, 'Bonica' haunted me because it was so agreeable. I decided to give it another try—in the landscape, where it was touted to outdo itself. It did, and two bushes I planted in a fallen tree stump bring traffic to a halt more than once a year. When it's in full bloom, you can barely spot foliage beneath the bounty of sprays of soft pink flowers.

I decided also to test the rose for other qualities it was purported to possess. Since the hybridizer (Meilland, of France) said it was disease resistant, I didn't spray it. Because claims were made that bushes need no pruning, I gave them none for more than five years. Quite handily, 'Bonica' passed all tests.

If you remember not to cut the last roses of summer, 'Bonica' will reward you with a bountiful crop of orange hips.

BRANDY

I don't believe I've ever met anyone (including hard-core rosarians) who doesn't like 'Brandy'. What's not to like? 'Brandy' is an elegant rose, in both its bloom and its bush, and the All-America Rose Selections organization recognized these qualities in 1982 by awarding Armstrong Nursery's Swim and Christensen for their Hybrid Tea beauty.

Beginning with its finest attribute, this rose's bloom is luxurious. The golden apricot petals (25–30 per bloom) are shapely, and blossoms display high centers and exhibition form. Fragrance is slight but sweet. Best yet, blooms appear at the tips of exceptionally long cutting stems.

Not only are bushes vigorous, they appreciate growing tall and production will increase if you prune accordingly (taller than most). Foliage is large and deep green. Bushes mature naturally into urn shapes, making them a pruner's dream.

Ideal Hybrid Tea rosebushes produce blossoms one to a stem. 'Brandy' epitomizes that quality and rarely needs disbudding. Another endearing quality (although you must admittedly be deeply into roses to appreciate it) is the color the canes turn in winter—deep russet brown. That may not seem like much until you learn that, in winter, rosebushes that distinguish themselves are a welcome relief to those charged with pruning them.

All matters considered, 'Brandy' is pure pleasure.

BRASS BAND

America's ace hybridizer Jack Christensen won an All-America award in 1995 for his Floribunda 'Brass Band', an award I applaud; as a judge, even voted for.

As judges, we're encouraged to write comments about the varieties we're considering for an award. Both years I grew 'Brass Band', I commented that in full bloom, bushes looked like a ladies lunch—short ladies, big hats. That very quality—a marked disparity between bush and bloom sizes—is what I believe makes 'Brass Band' such a winning rose. That, and the fact that it's such a happy rose.

You'd be happy, too, dressed up in these fruity colors—apricot, melon, and peach, with a lemon yellow petal reverse. Helped in part by sheer number (up to 35 per bloom), petals of 'Brass Band' compose large double blossoms that like to open fully (to the point of decadence, actually). In keeping with the color scheme, fragrance is also fruity.

Bushes of 'Brass Band' grow only to medium heights, but they are naturally well shaped and have a nice mounding growth habit. Foliage is bright green and glossy.

Whether or not you, too, believe plants in bloom resemble a ladies lunch, I'll bet you'll consider 'Brass Band' a worthy addition to the garden.

BRIGADOON

Of the roses mentioned in this book, more were hybridized by the late Bill Warriner of Jackson & Perkins fame than by any other rose breeder. 'Brigadoon', an All-America Hybrid Tea in 1992, was one of his last creations; it's also one of his finest.

Of all its many qualities, what separates 'Brigadoon' from its fine Hybrid Tea peers is its color. Classified by the American Rose Society as a pink blend, this selection's actual colors are far more complicated. First, petals aren't a single color but rather a blend graduating in intensity from tip to base. Second, colors pale in intensity during summer and fall. Finally, overall color defies categorization. Pink is there to be sure, but so are coral, rose, and cream, the combination of which is thoroughly pleasing, as is consistent fragrance from bud to buxom blossom.

Not only that, flowers are beautifully formed—high centered, urn shaped, and full petaled (35–40 per bloom). That 'Brigadoon' is a frequent visitor to awards tables at rose shows is no surprise, especially if you know that blooms usually come on long cutting stems.

Bushes are winning, too—upright but slightly spreading. In keeping with this rose's other fine attributes, foliage is dark green and semiglossy.

Ever since 'Bonica' became the first Landscape rose to win an All-America award, hybridizers have been eager to breed more of these easy-to-grow roses. In 1996 Francis Meilland of France, who hybridized 'Bonica', repeated his success with the All-America 'Carefree Delight'.

'Carefree Delight' is the quintessential Landscape rose, not only because it fits so well into the landscape but also, as advertised, because it's fuss-free. Foliage is small but dark glossy green and seemingly impervious to disease. Furthermore, as good Landscape roses should, blossoms look best when left in the garden. Tight little carmine-pink rosebuds open their five petals into lightish midpink blossoms that can each reach up to 3 inches across. Golden yellow stamens are smack-dab in the middle of a bright white eye. As final pluses, wood on 'Carefree Delight' turns a handsome shade of mahogany brown in winter—the same time the bush produces a smashing crop of hips.

Because judges at All-America Rose Selections Test Gardens are permitted to keep plants that are awarded, after growing 'Carefree Delight' as a test rose for two years, I then planted it near a picket fence at the bottom of my rose fields. Early each summer, those four bushes bring traffic to a firm halt as visitors gawk at the fluffy pink floral display. Passersby stop in their tracks again in fall, when the irresistible crop of hips showers plants. In short, 'Carefree Delight' is a joy year-round.

Some years ago, a survey was taken of San Francisco rosarians to learn which of the roses they grew were most disease resistant. 'Cathedral' was number one.

Bred by New Zealand's supertalented hybridizer Sam McGredy, 'Cathedral' was the Floribunda selected as All-America in 1976. It has remained a favorite of many rosarians ever since, and not simply because of its resistance to rose diseases.

The American Rose Society lists its color as an apricot blend because its petals are shades of apricot through salmon, but the overall impression one gets of its color is soft orange.

Although blooms of 'Cathedral' sometimes present themselves one to a stem (always, if you disbud for this look), they more frequently appear in sprays and, I think, look prettiest in such clusters. However they appear, individual blooms are fully double (22 petals each) and large for a Floribunda (to 5 inches across).

Foliage is olive green and notably glossy, and plants are bushy but nicely upright and contained, making 'Cathedral' a fine selection for growing in borders.

As a final plus, 'Cathedral' is particularly generous with its blossoms. Properly maintained and fertilized, bushes remain in constant bloom from early summer through late fall. In fact, it's rare to have no blossoms in evidence anytime throughout this period. Such reliability is a great bonus for those who want to enjoy their roses indoors.

COLOR MAGIC

Rosarians despise being asked to name their favorite rose, for it means choosing among a list of can't-do-withouts. When I could hedge no longer, I named 'Color Magic' my favorite. It has everything I want in a modern rose—rich colors, delicious fragrance, and dinner-plate-size blooms.

When Jackson & Perkins' indefatigable hybridizer Bill Warriner introduced 'Spellbinder' in 1975, I knew he was onto something great. Three years later, he crossed 'Spellbinder' with an unknown seedling and hit the jackpot with 'Color Magic'. He won an All-America Selection award in 1978 for that particular effort.

The bloom's basic color is apricot pink, but this Hybrid Tea is truly a blend, with colors ranging from dark rose-pink to a rich buff-beige center. The size is simply staggering, and the more blooms open, the more beautiful they become. Fully open blossoms will easily fill a 9-inch space, and the exhibition stage between half and three-quarters open is a sight to behold.

I think I can identify 'Color Magic' blindfolded by its fragrance alone. It has that quality some call classic Tea scent, but it's strong and full bodied. Stems are long and large, and if you can grow the bush well, you must treat it harshly to keep gargantuan growth from developing—not a casual challenge, since you, too, are bound to want as many blossoms as possible from this fabulous rose.

DOUBLE DELIGHT

I saw a photograph of this rose before seeing the bloom itself and was sure that the suppliers were playing a trick on us. 'Double Delight' is indeed something else. Blooms really are red and white, and the colors are dramatically combined, with red sprawling irregularly over white petals. Sun and variable weather conditions produce different color patterns, so no two blooms are ever exactly alike. Add to this a strong fragrance and great form, and it's clear why 'Double Delight' is so popular. It was selected as an All-America Rose for 1977 and quickly became a favorite among exhibition roses.

The bush is strong and produces an amazing number of blooms. Although all degrees of openness are nice, the exhibition stage is best. Blossoms of 'Double Delight' are also perfectly wonderful when fully open, and the colors remain strong, as does the spicy fragrance. Medium green foliage is abundant but otherwise not particularly notable.

Three years after it introduction, 'Double Delight' produced an offspring, 'Mon Cheri', which, although not quite as impressive as its parent, is also a wonderful rose, especially if you prefer pink rather than white combined with red. Blossoms are fragrant, large, and produced in great quantities on a bush quite similar to that of its predecessor. 'Mon Cheri' also copped an All-America award (1982).

A climbing version of 'Double Delight' is now commercially available for those of you who might want to splash your garden walls or trellis with red and white.

D U E T

Once, for lack of something better to do, I kept count of every rose produced on every rose-bush in my private San Francisco garden. 'Duet', a notorious workhorse among roses, was the hands-down winner.

An All-America Selection in 1961, 'Duet' was introduced as a Grandiflora because of its proclivity for producing multiple blooms on one stem. Later it was reclassified as a Hybrid Tea (a classification I endorse). No one bothered to explain the change to 'Duet', however, and it can't seem to resist the urge to produce multiple blossoms on each stem rather than the one-to-a-stem blooms of classic Hybrid Tea roses. Never mind; it's a winner any way it presents itself.

The American Rose Society classifies 'Duet' as medium pink, but it's actually a blend since each blossom's 25–30 petals are light pink on the inside but dark pink outside—a winning combination. The ample foliage, produced on vigorous upright bushes, is shiny, dark green, and leathery; best of all, it's disease resistant. Although fragrance is no stronger than moderate, it's crisp and clean. As a final plus, the blooms last particularly well (on the bush or in a vase).

The only people I've ever heard complain about 'Duet' are florists who say that blooms resemble each other more than do the blossoms of any other single rose variety. Sorry; I feel no sympathy for such nitpicking. 'Duet' is a rosarian's rose, and a fine one at that.

E U R O P E A N A

Why it took 'Europeana' five years to reach American shores after de Ruiter of Holland hybridized it in 1963, I'm not quite sure. It was an All-America Selection for 1968 and has since endeared itself with two characteristics that will keep it in the Floribunda forefront for a long time to come. First, its color. There are lots of reds, but not enough rubies. 'Europeana' is a dark red that holds its color from start to finish. Second, 'Europeana' is the most exemplary Floribunda I know for geometric inflorescences of multiple blooms on one stem, rather than blossoms placed randomly here and there. 'Europeana' read the show rules and took them to heart. You still have to remove the terminal bud, but once you do, sit back in confident anticipation of a great spray of bloom.

If the color and size work for you, 'Europeana' is a terrific landscape rose. It's low growing, almost as wide as tall, and clothed in glossy dark green foliage that retains strong hints of mahogany. Blossom fragrance is light but definite.

I must admit that I didn't like 'Europeana' when I first saw it. Rosette-shaped blooms weren't what I was looking for. Now 'Europeana' has grown on me, and I see why it's such a great rose.

F A M E !

Exclamation mark or not, you're likely to shout when you see 'Fame!', the All-America award-winning Grandiflora for 1998. I knew this rose was destined for stardom the first year I grew it in the test garden. It was one of those roses that all but said "Choose me, I'm the winner." Although I liked it from our first meeting, my appreciation deepened during the second year. By fall, bushes had matured beautifully and gave freely of some of the most perfectly formed blossoms the test garden had ever produced.

Proud of its color, 'Fame!' lets it all hang out where pink is concerned. Even people who claim they don't like strong pink somehow make an exception where 'Fame!' is concerned. Maybe it's the incredibly formed mature flowers that make people so want this rose. I predict that 'Fame!' is bound to be a superstar, at least on awards tables at rose exhibitions. Mature blossoms are pure perfection—pinpoint centers with 30–35 frilly petals unfurling uniformly around them.

When its blooms occur one to a stem, they're knockouts. Far more frequently, blossoms are in sprays of three to five flowers each; they, too, are lovely. Bushes are vigorous and particularly well branched. More than anything else, however, they're stubbornly floriferous.

When Keith Zary took on hybridizing for Jackson & Perkins, he had a pair of mighty shoes to fill—those owned by his predecessor, William Warriner. With 'Fame!', Zary shows rosedom his intention to man the job.

FIRST PRIZE

There was only one All-America Rose Selection in 1970, probably because nothing else could stand up to hybridizer Gene Boerner's 'First Prize' to share the honors. Once 'First Prize' was introduced, it cut a beeline for the list of top Hybrid Tea exhibition roses. Today 'First Prize' enjoys an 8.6 rating by the American Rose Society, placing it strongly among "excellent" roses, very close to "outstanding."

'First Prize' is a fabulous rose for lots of reasons, one being its fantastic blend of colors. It starts out as a high-centered pink, but with deep pink outer petals. Before it has finished opening, beige becomes the center's major color. Blooms reach amazing proportions with only 25 petals, probably because not a single one is misplaced in the creation of classic Hybrid Tea form.

The bush on which 'First Prize' sports its lovely blossoms is vigorous and upright, and foliage is dark green and leathery. Although it has a tendency to mildew, when the bush produces blossoms the size of dinner plates, it's easy to forgive such a fault.

For the first few years I grew 'First Prize', I thought it scentless; then one day I got a hint of its perfume. Other people I know still detect no fragrance. If you're after strong scent, don't plant 'First Prize'. If you think you might someday like to exhibit your roses, don't even consider doing without it.

F R E N C H   L A C E

Because I grow garden roses for the sale of their cut blossoms to the floral trade, I'm forced to pay attention to the buying trends of florists across the country. "No oranges in spring, no pinks in fall," they say to me as though I have seasonal powers to make roses bloom in specific colors.

I never fret over when 'French Lace' blossoms, however, because its blooms sell any time of the year, even to customers who weren't thinking about pastel roses when they called to order. Two reasons explain the enormous popularity of this 1982 All-America Floribunda— yet another jeweled trophy for the late, great hybridizer William Warriner.

First, color. Petals range from pale apricot at their bases to white at their tips, ivory in between—a color range found in fine porcelains.

Second, form. I've sat in lost wonder gazing at a spray of 'French Lace' while pretending that I'm a snotty rose judge at the toughest of rose shows, trying to find fault. Often, I can't.

Although 'French Lace' sometimes produces a single bloom per stem, more often they're in clusters from as few as 3 to as many as 12. Fragrance is slight but sweet.

Bushes are moderately vigorous, and foliage is small and dark.

All elements considered, 'French Lace' is a breathtaking beauty.

'Golden Showers', hybridized by America's Walter Lammerts, was the very first Climbing rose to win an All-America award, which it did in 1957. (There have been only two other Climbing roses to walk away with the honor since, and one won't be introduced into commerce until fall 1999.)

If 'Golden Showers' is nothing else, it's decidedly yellow—specifically, daffodil yellow, according to the American Rose Society. Better yet, its blooms are richly fragrant and its plants agreeably vigorous. Although usually grown as a conventional arching climber, 'Golden Showers' will also grow straight up, making it a fine selection for gardeners who yearn for a pillar rose. In either case, when blossoming occurs, blooms shower plants from top to bottom.

Buds are long, pointed, and high centered, but the mature blossoms of approximately 27 petals each are rather flat and up to 4 inches across; they're also decidedly fragrant at all stages, whether they occur one to a stem or in large clusters. Foliage is not only abundant, it's also dark and glossy.

Many Climbing roses are stingy with their blossoms after the first flush of blooms in early summer, but not 'Golden Showers', which repeats its blossoming regularly throughout summer. The majority of plants of 'Golden Showers' reach heights of only 6–7 feet. When they're contented with full sun and ample water and fertilizers, however, expect heights of 10–12 feet. In full flower, mature plants showered in eye-blinking golden yellow are visible from great distances.

GRANADA

'Granada', an All-America Selection Hybrid Tea from hybridizer Robert Lindquist in 1964, is as popular today as it was when it was introduced. That's because it possesses two fundamental requirements for an immortal rose: it's a blooming fool and intensely fragrant at all stages of development.

Often called the "birthday cake rose" because of its resemblance to confectionary roses used with icings to decorate baked goods, 'Granada' is a wondrous blend of colors—vermilion, nasturtium red, and lemon yellow, the combination of which yields an eye-blinking fluorescent quality. Buds are attractively urn shaped and can be cut tight; they'll always open, and the colors will intensify.

A bush of 'Granada' can be identified even without blooms; plants are of low to medium height and clothed in somewhat crinkled foliage that is leathery and distinctly toothed. Often another distinguishing characteristic is a set of highly decorative sepals (the leaflike structures just under the buds and above the foliage), which can be amazingly long, elegantly framing the blooms.

'Granada' has another endearing trait—it is the first rose to bloom in most gardens of modern roses. Understand that when roses finally bloom in spring, weeks after you wish they had, the first bloom is a welcome sight indeed. Then, too, there's that ravishing fragrance to remind you of what you can look forward to sniffing all summer long.

HONOR

In 1980 Jackson & Perkins' indefatigable Bill Warriner made a clean sweep of the All-America Selections, winning the Floribunda category with 'Cherish', the Grandiflora class with 'Love', and the Hybrid Tea award with 'Honor'.

For reasons best known to me at the time (of which I have no good recollection now), I looked down my nose at 'Honor', claiming that it was just another white Hybrid Tea, nothing special. Boy, was I wrong! In marked contrast, I now believe 'Honor' is one of the finest Hybrid Tea roses ever hybridized.

If height is of concern to you and your garden, you should know that a bush of 'Honor' is a potential skyscraper—as tall as any white Hybrid Tea I've ever grown. That's not a disadvantage, of course, merely a forewarning. On the plus side, the tall bushes are extremely well shaped and a pruner's delight because they seem to yearn to grow into the classic urn shape that is so desirous for modern roses. Foliage is large and deep green.

The blossoms, however, are the ticket—pure white, elegantly pointed in bud, fully double (23 petals), and nicely fragrant for a pure white rose. Stems are exceptionally long, and blooms last well as cut flowers.

I retract every single ugly remark I ever made about 'Honor'; it's a great rose.

INTRIGUE

Talk about a rose not meant for everyone, 'Intrigue' never draws ambivalent comments—entirely due to its color, purple. (The American Rose Society has it registered as mauve, but that's because they don't have a category for reddish purple; if they did, 'Intrigue' would be accurately listed.)

Although several heirloom roses were purple, the color didn't begin appearing in modern roses until the latter half of the 20th century. When first introduced, they were insanely popular. Two decades later they went out of fashion, and they have only lately regained popularity. 'Intrigue', from the hands of Jackson & Perkins' formidable hybridizer Bill Warriner and an All-America winning Floribunda in 1984, is a good example of why purple roses are on the rebound.

With only 20 petals each, individual blossoms of 'Intrigue' manage to mature into large flowers that prefer appearing in sprays (rather than one to a stem). Like most modern roses in the mauve family, 'Intrigue' is richly fragrant.

Plants are also worth writing about—vigorous (especially for a Floribunda), upright yet bushy, and well clothed in dark green, semiglossy foliage. Prune 'Intrigue' more severely than you do most Floribundas and you'll be delighted with the prolific, long-stemmed, richly perfumed sprays that are destined to follow.

MEDALLION

I'm annoyed that 'Medallion', an All-America Hybrid Tea rose for 1973, isn't highly rated by the American Rose Society, especially that the members don't look upon it more favorably (its mature blossoms are oversized, a quality I admire). When someone tells me they want to grow a huge, fragrant rose of a smart color, I unhesitatingly suggest 'Medallion'—yet another winner from Jackson & Perkins' star hybridizer Bill Warriner.

Apricot varieties were popular as old roses, but they came a little late in the hybridizing of modern roses. Once they caught on and there were plenty for parenting, however, apricots and their blends gained rapidly in popularity. Almost all are fragrant.

'Medallion' is a nice bush, too. It's vigorous, tall, shapely, and covered in medium green foliage. It has a spreading quality that's nice for keeping long-stemmed roses out of each other's way.

The buds are exceptionally long, and you must wait for more than unfurled sepals before cutting this bloom. The bud itself must begin unfurling and show its first row of petals clearly apart from the center before you take the bloom from its bush, or 'Medallion' won't open. Taken from the bush at the right time, it may well get to be the biggest rose you've ever seen.

M I S T E R   L I N C O L N

The great American hybridizing duo of Swim and Weeks crossed 'Chrysler Imperial' and 'Charles Mallerin' to get two wonderful, dark red Hybrid Tea seedlings for introduction in 1964. One was 'Mister Lincoln', the other 'Oklahoma'.

In 1965 'Mister Lincoln' won an All-America award. Today it's rated 8.6 (10.0 is perfect) by the American Rose Society, and it has become the favorite dark red rose of the majority of rosarians in the world. This hardy, robust rose is long on fragrance.

Blossoms of 'Mister Lincoln' should always be grown one to a stem. Fortunately, that is easy to do, since new growth needs disbudding less often than that on most Hybrid Teas. Not only is the bush of 'Mister Lincoln' a prolific bloomer, it also has a nice habit of growing upright and can be readily pruned to the classic urn shape.

I can't count the number of people who have asked me if I've seen the "black rose," then gone on to argue when I claim it doesn't exist. 'Mister Lincoln' is as black as I care a red rose to be while it's in bud. As it opens, the center petalage proves to be a much lighter, cherry red, and it's intensely fragrant all the while. Admittedly, 'Mister Lincoln' has a tendency to "blue" toward the end of its very long vase life. But let's give it a break. No rose has yet earned a perfect 10.0.

OLYMPIAD

In 1984 New Zealand's creative hybridizer Sam McGredy won an All-America award for his dazzling red Hybrid Tea. In return, and in honor of the Olympic Summer Games in Los Angeles the same year, he named his beauty 'Olympiad'.

Honesty compels me to tell you at the getgo that the single flaw 'Olympiad' possesses is lack of fragrance, and I don't mean "slight" fragrance; I mean not a whiff. If you can forgive the rose for this omission (as in always using it in arrangements that include strongly perfumed varieties, so that no one will notice its scentlessness), there are attributes worth talking about—namely, color and form.

'Olympiad' is truly red, as brilliantly purely colored as any rose of any age. Form is nothing short of exemplary. Because its blossoms of 35 petals each are fully double, 'Olympiad' can afford to play with petal placement; it almost always decides to go for perfection. An exhibitor's dream, three-quarters-open blossoms have bull's-eye centers with petals unfurling perfectly symmetrically around them.

Bushes are noticeably different from those of most modern Hybrid Teas, especially in their foliage, which is matte, medium to lightish green and widely spaced.

Another unique quality is how a bush of 'Olympiad' can be treated at pruning time—harshly. Because it vastly prefers blooming on new (rather than second-year) wood, plants can be pruned hard. New, strong growth is guaranteed. Put some effort into forgiving this rose's embarrassing lack of aroma. I have, and I'm over it.

PARADISE

Here's a Hybrid Tea toward which hardly anyone is ambivalent. For some, it's a color too weird to have around. For others, it's too amazing to live without. Whichever, I wish I had hybridized it, but Ollie Weeks did, and earned an All-America Rose Selection in 1979. It's silvery lavender, splashed with ruby red on the petal edges and in random blotches into the bloom. Besides being one of the most unusual color combinations in modern rosedom, it's fragrant. Finally, it has downright incredible form. Even the smallest of blooms will have 26–30 petals perfectly arranged around a bull's-eye center. In fact, I know few roses that can match 'Paradise' for consistent exhibition form.

Bushes are tall and upright. Although foliage is a rather noncommittal shade of green, it's at least abundant and well spaced.

'Paradise' fits quite nicely into one of the latest additions to the color-classification system of the American Rose Society—mauve blend. If you had seen it in a rose show before this class was available, your natural tendency would have been to move it someplace else. Now it will seem at home with the likes of 'Patsy Cline', 'Escapade', 'Silver Star', 'Silverado', and other roses that perform well at the show table. I predict that other roses soon to be hybridized will quickly join this color class—it's popular right now, and those who like it get to be nuts about it.

PASCALI

I have a friend who has only white flowers in his garden. Half of them are roses, and they're almost all 'Pascali'. It's *the* white rose if you want purity with no shadings of color.

Hybridized by Lens in 1963, this is the only rose of international importance from Belgium. The name is synonymous with Easter, and the rose was selected as All-America in 1969. Where it grows well, it performs wonderfully.

Often when I cut a bloom of 'Pascali', I complain that it's too small. Some days later (when it has actually grown in its vase), I take back what I said. The blooms almost always have classic form, rarely with split centers.

When you compare this bush with other Hybrid Teas, the stems appear weak and unable to support a large bloom, even one with only 30 petals. But they are strong and prove to be more supportive than larger, thicker stems. Then, too, the diameter of the stems must lend itself well to drawing water, since blooms last amazingly well. The current rating by the American Rose Society of 8.1 is well deserved, and 'Pascali' is among the top exhibition roses in the United States.

Of all the white Hybrid Tea roses I grow, 'Pascali' is probably the most popular with florists. They don't always realize that the reason they like the foliage is that 'Pascali' is so disease resistant. They know well, however, that 'Pascali' is a superb cut flower with an unusually extended vase life.

PEACE

The arrival of the 'Peace' rose could not have been more perfectly timed to make it the most famous rose in the world. It was the ultimate accomplishment of its hybridizer, Francis Meilland of France, and its budwood was spirited from France on some of the last planes to leave before the World War II occupation. The rose survived to become the floral symbol of the United Nations' formation in San Francisco in 1946 and was the All-America Selection the same year. Today it remains one of the top exhibition roses in the United States.

I think of 'Peace' as yellow, although it's classified by the American Rose Society as a blend. In fact, no two blooms are alike, and this is part of its enduring charm. I've seen the basic color so pale that it's really off-white, with edges dipped in pink. Sometimes, though, usually in the fall, its color is a deep clear yellow turning to coral-orange at petal edges.

Here's a rose I definitely like better past the bud stage, preferably three-quarters open. The color variations add to its appeal for exhibition, and its form can be exemplary. 'Peace' is considered slightly fragrant, though this is hardly why you'd grow it. Bushes grow strongly to medium heights, foliage is dark and shiny, and flowers should be grown for one bloom per stem (sprays are disappointing by comparison).

'Peace' is certain to remain a favorite forever, if for sentimental reasons alone.

PERFECT MOMENT

The Kordes clan in Germany have given the rose world many fine varieties, including 'Iceberg', arguably the finest rose in the world. A more recent contribution is 'Perfect Moment', an All-America Hybrid Tea Selection in 1991.

When you tell people about a good red-and-yellow rose you know, they often look dubious, as though you surely meant another color scheme. Harsh combination? Not the way 'Perfect Moment' puts these hues together.

The reason 'Perfect Moment' presents such an eye-blinking color scheme is not simply that petals combine red and yellow, it's the way they do it. Individual petals are red on their inner upper reaches and yellow toward their inner bases. To keep color in perpetual motion, the red-and-yellow scheme is reversed on the petals' outsides. As if 'Perfect Moment' read somewhere how well-mannered Hybrid Teas are supposed to present their blossoms, flowers almost always appear one to a stem. Form is of exhibition quality, and fragrance is fruity and crisp.

As with many Kordes roses, bushes grow to medium-tall heights and are strong, vigorous, and well clothed in dark green, semiglossy foliage that is leathery and resistant to disease. Cutting stems are admirably long and graceful.

Q U E E N   E L I Z A B E T H

When 'Queen Elizabeth' was presented to the rose world, it created such a stir that a whole new class of roses was created for it—Grandiflora. Bred by the great American hybridizer Walter Lammerts in 1954, 'Queen Elizabeth' was the All-America Selection for 1955. Three decades later, it was voted the world's favorite rose by the World Federation of Rose Societies. Today it still ranks as one of the top exhibition roses in the Grandiflora class.

The numerous plaudits bestowed on 'Queen Elizabeth' are well deserved, since it is indeed a regal bush and bloom. The Queen is a very tall grower and shouldn't be coerced into shorter heights by pruning too low, or she will spend most of the following growing season reaching the height at which she blooms comfortably.

If your landscape has height limitations, plant another rose. If you can respect its lofty habits, 'Queen Elizabeth' will reward you with panicles of rose- and dawn pink blooms of 37–40 petals each, occurring mostly in clusters. Disbudding should be geared toward producing these multiple blooms on one stem. The bush will stubbornly produce single blooms no matter what you do, and they're pretty, but sprays are more impressive, and once bushes are established, you can easily cut inflorescences with 2- to 3-foot stems. Foliage is large, dark, glossy, and leathery.

Besides its stately bush, the disease resistance of 'Queen Elizabeth' is a great plus, as is its vigor—two reasons it still enjoys a respectable rating by the voting members of the American Rose Society. The Queen is in no imminent danger of being dethroned.

I'm generally not fond of roses in bud, preferring blooms after they're about halfway open. Here, however, is the exception. There's no more elegant bud in all of rosedom than that of 'Royal Highness'. It's frosty pink (about as light as it could be and still be classified as pink), and 'Royal Highness' was the first Hybrid Tea of this color to be selected as All-America. It was chosen in 1963 and has reigned majestically ever since.

'Royal Highness' has a number of appealing qualities, starting with an affinity for one-to-a-stem growth. Stems are long and cloaked in dark green foliage that looks as though it's impervious to disease (alas, it's somewhat prone to powdery mildew). Although the open bloom of 'Royal Highness' can be a little loose, verging on blowsy, it's always pretty. Fragrance is light but somehow fitting for this color.

The bush is about as classic as the bud. It's tall, upright, and almost naturally urn shaped, making pruning easy. Although bushes prefer growing tall, they're obedient to hard pruning, which encourages long-stemmed beauties.

'Royal Highness' is yet another winner from the American hybridizing team of Swim and Weeks. Although it has lost its patent (roses are patented for only 17 years), 'Royal Highness' is destined to stay around until something worthy (and identically colored) takes its place—a day not yet in clear sight.

S A R A T O G A

America's Gene Boerner bred so many winning Floribunda roses that he earned the nickname "Papa Floribunda." 'Saratoga' is one of his triumphs.

An All-America Selection in 1964, 'Saratoga' is an exemplary Floribunda, producing scads of off-white blossoms in irregular sprays. Buds are ovoid, but mature blossoms are fully double (33 petals each) and shaped like gardenias. Fragrance is notable, particularly for a white rose.

Plants are thoroughly agreeable, too—vigorous, bushy, and upright. Foliage is glossy and leathery.

'Saratoga' is a fine selection for gardeners interested in enjoying their roses as cut flowers. Not only do blossoms last well in a vase, they mix well with roses of all colors. And, of course, there's that fragrance that can be relied upon, especially important when other roses in a mixed bouquet may not have notable perfume.

You need to read up on disbudding techniques if you intend to enjoy 'Saratoga' as a cut flower. Because sprays are large, they'll always include a terminal bud (the largest in a collection of buds at the end of a stem). If terminal buds are removed as soon as they are obvious (they'll be noticeably larger than any of the others), the remaining buds will mature evenly into massive white sprays.

Although I usually recommend no more than moderate pruning for Floribunda roses, because of its astounding vigor I suggest you consider pruning 'Saratoga' hard—a sure ticket to strong-stemmed, weighty sprays.

Californian Tom Carruth presented the rose world with a fine gift by hybridizing 'Scentimental'. That it won a Floribunda All-America award in 1997 came as no surprise to anyone who saw it under cultivation in test gardens around the country; it was a star from the time of its first bloom.

Besides its considerable beauty, 'Scentimental' makes an even broader contribution to rosedom because it just may prove to be what it takes to unite two hardheaded groups of rosarians who never see eye to eye—those devoted to antique roses because of their whimsical form and fragrance, and those who prefer modern hybrids because they blossom throughout summer. 'Scentimental' pleases everyone; it looks and smells for all the world like an antique rose, but it blooms nonstop.

'Scentimental' is wondrously colored. Petals are deep hot pink shaded rose, splashed with creamy to pure white random striations. Fragrance is deep and strong. Although blossoms occasionally appear one to a stem, more frequently they occur in large sprays with ample cutting stems. Blooms last well on or off the bush, and colors intensify as they mature.

Bushes are exceptionally well behaved and as resistant to disease as any modern rose, which is a blessing because you'd want nothing to impair the luscious foliage that looks like finely tooled dark green leather. On behalf of rosarians worldwide, thank you, Tom Carruth; 'Scentimental' is a true-blue winner.

SHEER BLISS

When Bill Warriner introduced 'Pristine' in 1978, I was convinced that I wouldn't look seriously at another white rose with pink edges for a long time to come. Nine years later, Warriner proved me wrong when his Hybrid Tea 'Sheer Bliss' won an All-America award.

Considering that its blossoms are elegantly delicate, you might expect fragile bushes. Quite the contrary. Bushes of 'Sheer Bliss' are vigorous and like growing tall. Canes are thick, and stems are long and strong. Healthy foliage is often oversized and deep, deep green.

With all due credit to its growth habits, the blooms of 'Sheer Bliss' are the secret to its success—namely, their color and form.

The American Rose Society classifies 'Sheer Bliss' as white, but it's actually much more; pinkish white outer petals tinged deeper pink. As blooms mature, colors lighten but never turn pure white.

Maturing blossoms of 'Sheer Bliss' have classic exhibition form. Unlike most show roses, three-quarters-open flowers are more oval than round. Centers are pinpoint.

Considering that many near-white roses don't have notable fragrance, 'Sheer Bliss' is a welcome exception. The sweet perfume is fruity and crisp. Stem length is outrageous.

SHEER ELEGANCE

I'm a critic of many rose names because they often have nothing whatsoever to do with the rose itself. 'Sheer Elegance', however, deservedly fits its name and merits its 1991 All-America award.

Blossom color is most elegant of all—orange-pink, according to the American Rose Society, but for most of the season the blooms in my garden have little if any orange. Pink is more like it, darkest at the petals' edges, with soft pastel gradations in between.

Because blossoms boast up to 43 petals each, 'Sheer Elegance' can afford to be prissy in arranging them, which it does—pinpoint, bullet centers with rows of petals unfurling symmetrically around them. What with all the fuss about color and form, you might imagine that perfume is lacking. It's not.

Bushes are elegant, too; at least as much as bushes of modern roses ever are. Growth is upright, urn shaped, and vigorous. Similarly, foliage is large, glossy, and often as russet-red as it is emerald green.

Few roses mix in arrangements as comfortably as 'Sheer Elegance'. Its colors blend well with almost every rose nearby, and its picture-perfect form and dependable fresh fragrance are always a plus.

Kudos to America's hybridizer Bill Twomey of DeVor Nursery.

People constantly ask me to recommend a brown rose. For years, I could tell them only about 'Julia's Rose', a variety I wouldn't grow if you paid me—incredibly stingy blossoms on a puny bush. Then, in 1995, New Zealand's Sam McGredy copped yet another All-America award in recognition of his stunning Floribunda 'Singin' in the Rain'. Now I could honestly recommend a "brown" rose.

Please understand that 'Singin' in the Rain' isn't entirely brown. Nice parchment brown is certainly present, but so is cinnamon-pink. Then, too, colors alter slightly during the year—fading in summer, intensifying in fall. However the blooms choose to transform their colors, several times a year you'll say "Look at that brown rose" and actually mean it.

Rather tall for a Floribunda, 'Singin' in the Rain' bushes are masked in dark green, glossy leaves that show marked resistance to disease. Flowering is steady throughout summer and fragrance is sweet. One-to-a-stem blooms appear occasionally; more frequently, blossoms are formed in sprays of three to five flowers each.

Befitting its name, 'Singin' in the Rain' is a happy rose.

T I F F A N Y

No one quibbles over the appropriateness of 'Tiffany' as the name of one of the world's most elegant Hybrid Tea roses. It's entirely believable that had Louis Comfort Tiffany been a rose hybridizer rather than a fine glass artisan, he would have selected this very rose to bear his surname.

Hybridized by America's Robert Lindquist in 1954, 'Tiffany' was an All-America Selection in 1955, the same year it copped a Gold Medal award in the Portland rose trials. Since then, it has won numerous honors, including those given exclusively for fragrance.

Everything about 'Tiffany' exudes elegance, beginning with its long pointed bud composed of 28 petals not unlike those Tiffany used in his stained glass representations of roses. Style is maintained well past the bud stage—throughout bloom life, in fact, concluding with fully double blossoms that reach up to 5 inches across. Ravishing classic rose fragrance is present at all stages.

Bushes are well shaped, too. Not only are they tall, they're also staunchly upright, vigorous, and clothed in dark green foliage that perfectly complements the delicately colored blossoms—technically a blend (because yellow is present at the base of each petal) but primarily soft pink.

Four years after its introduction as a bush, 'Tiffany' became available as a climber. Grown either way, it exhibits blossoms that are studies in perfection.

TOUCH OF CLASS

Despite its elitist name and thoroughly prissy form, I must admit that 'Touch of Class' is indeed a classy Hybrid Tea. The French certainly thought so when hybridizer Kriloff introduced it as 'Maréchal le Clerc' in 1984 and so did Americans in 1986 when it won an All-America award and acquired its present name.

Before reading another word, be forewarned that 'Touch of Class' has no fragrance whatsoever. The best it ever smells is "clean," which it is.

Blossoms, however, tell quite another story. 'Touch of Class' puts its blooms to the test of perfect petal arrangement and they pass muster, with 30-odd petals unfurling around a high-centered, exhibition-quality flower. The American Rose Society has registered 'Touch of Class' as orange-pink (personally, I believe orange alone would do; true, the orange coloring is soft, but it's still resolutely orange).

Bushes are upright growers and prefer to be left tall after pruning. The dark green foliage is notably large and semiglossy.

'Touch of Class' enjoys a 9.3 rating from the American Rose Society, so voting members have obviously forgiven 'Touch of Class' for its scentlessness. You will, too, if you decide to add it to your garden.

William Warriner of Jackson & Perkins made his name famous among rose lovers primarily for the creation of lovely Hybrid Teas. With 'Tournament of Roses', he extended his talents to the Grandiflora class, and won an All-America award in 1989. His effort is indeed worthy of a rose celebration and a fitting tribute to the 100th anniversary of the world-renowned parade.

Two-tone roses often attain their finest stage of beauty when petals are one color on the inside and another on the reverse side. 'Tournament of Roses' is exemplary in such gradations of color, combining coral-pink with rose-pink (darker on the outside).

Although they occasionally occur one to a stem, more frequently blooms are carried in sprays of three to six flowers each. Individual blossoms are fully double (35–40 petals each), high centered, and large (to 4 inches across). Fragrance is light but spicy.

Bushes are exceptionally well behaved. They're vigorous but upright, and the semi-glossy foliage is large, dark green, and adamantly resistant to disease.

An extremely floriferous variety, 'Tournament of Roses' displays blossoms that improve in color as the weather warms (those gardening where winters are bitter should also know that 'Tournament of Roses' is thoroughly winter-hardy).

WHITE LIGHTNIN'

In 1981, when Armstrong Nursery's Swim and Christensen's 'White Lightnin'' became the first white Grandiflora to win an All-America award, it seemed on the road to stardom. Today it labors under a low rating by the American Rose Society, but please don't let that keep you from growing this good rose. I believe the low rating is due to the fact that the majority of rosarians who take the time to rate roses are deeply interested in exhibiting their wares and 'White Lightnin'' doesn't fare well in rose shows because the poor thing was misclassified to begin with. It should have been registered as a Floribunda—give it a break.

Whatever the causes for the disparaging rating, I couldn't agree with it less, and neither will you when you cut the blooms it gives so freely. The mother of 'White Lightnin'' is 'Angel Face'. You can see the familial resemblance when you compare the blooms of the two varieties. 'White Lightnin'' has wavy petals like those of its female parent. Also like 'Angel Face', it has great fragrance, in this case a unique, quite citruslike scent.

The bush is of medium height (short for a Grandiflora), and foliage is dark and glossy.

'White Lightnin'' is a blooming fool, and both sprays and one-to-a-stem blooms appear simultaneously. Form is terrific either way.

Official   All-America   Rose   Selections
Test   Gardens

Brigham Young University
267 WIDB
Provo, Utah 84602
Frank Williams, Judge
(801) 378-2760

Chicago Botanic Gardens
1000 Lake-Cook Road
Glenco, Illinois 60022
Eileen Byrne, Judge
(847) 835-5440

City of Buffalo/Joan Fuzak Memorial Garden
502 City Hall
Buffalo, New York 14202
Stan Swisher, Judge
(716) 851-4268

Descanso Gardens
1418 Descanso Drive
La Canada Flintridge, California 91011
Mary Brosius, Judge
(818) 952-4396

Disney Institute
Gardening & The Great Outdoors
Program Administration Building
1901 Buena Vista Drive
Lake Buena Vista, Florida 32830
Laura Coar, Judge
(407) 824-7131

Doane College
1014 Boswell
Crete, Nebraska 68333
Debra Khouri, Judge
(402) 826-2161

Edisto Gardens
620 Middleton Street
Orangeburg, South Carolina 29115
Rudy Groomes, Judge
(803) 533-5870

E.F.A. Reinisch Rose Test Garden
4320 West 10th
Topeka, Kansas 66604
Robert Foster, Judge
(913) 272-6150

Elizabeth Park Rose Garden
150 Walbridge Road
West Hartford, Connecticut 06119
Donna Fuss, Judge
(860) 243-1586

Fernbank Science Center
156 Heaton Park Drive, NE
Atlanta, Georgia 30307
Connie Kneisel, Judge
(404) 378-4311

Garden Valley Ranch
498 Pepper Road
Petaluma, California 94952
Rayford Reddell, Judge
(707) 795-0919

International Rose Test Gardens
400 S.W. Kingston Avenue
Portland, Oregon 97201
Harry Landers, Judge
(503) 823-3636

Iowa State University
141 Horticulture Building
Ames, Iowa 50011
Jeff Iles, Judge
(515) 294-0029

John E. Voight Trial Garden
Boerner Botanical Gardens
5879 S. 92nd Street
Hales Corners, Wisconsin 53130
William Radler, Judge
(414) 425-1131

Lyndale Park Gardens
3800 Bryant Avenue, South
Minneapolis, Minnesota 55409
Mary Lerman, Judge
(612) 370-4900

Michigan State University
Department of Horticulture
East Lansing, Michigan 48824
Douglas Badgero, Judge
(517) 353-4800

Missouri Botanical Gardens
4344 Shaw Boulevard
St. Louis, Missouri 63110
Barbara Hamilton, Judge
(314) 577-5190

Norfolk Botanical Garden
Azaleas Garden Road
Norfolk, Virginia 23518
Alan L. Lutz, Judge
(757) 441-5830

Old Westbury Gardens
71 Old Westbury Road
Old Westbury, L.I., New York 11568
Nelson Sterner, Judge
(516) 333-0048

Tyler Municipal Rose Garden
420 S. Rose Park Drive
Tyler, Texas 75702
John Seiover, Judge
(903) 531-1213

Woodland Park Rose Garden
5500 Phinney Avenue, North
Seattle, Washington 98103
Robert Lasser, Judge
(206) 684-4863

Woodward Park
1370 E. 24th Place
Tulsa, Oklahoma 74114
Rodney Bennett, Judge
(918) 596-7275

APPENDIX B

All - America Rose Selections

1 9 4 0
'Dickson's Red'
'Flash'
'The Chief'
'World's Fair'

1 9 4 1
'Apricot Queen'
'California'
'Charlotte Armstrong'

1 9 4 2
'Heart's Desire'

1 9 4 3
'Grande Duchesse Charlotte'
'Mary Margaret McBride'

1 9 4 4
'Fred Edmunds'
'Katherine T. Marshall'
'Lowell Thomas'
'Mme Chiang Kai-shek'
'Mme Marie Curie'

1 9 4 5
'Floradora'
'Horace McFarland'
'Mirandy'

1 9 4 6
'Peace'

1 9 4 7
'Rubaiyat'

1 9 4 8
'Diamond Jubilee'
'High Noon'
'Nocturne'
'Pinkie'
'San Fernando'
'Taffeta'

1 9 4 9
'Forty-niner'
'Tallyho'

1 9 5 0
'Capistrano'
'Fashion'
'Mission Bells'
'Sutter's Gold'

1 9 5 1
No selection

1 9 5 2
'Fred Howard'
'Helen Traubel'
'Vogue'

1 9 5 3
'Chrysler Imperial'
'Ma Perkins'

1 9 5 4
'Lilibet'
'Mojave'

1 9 5 5
'Jiminy Cricket'
'Queen Elizabeth'
'Tiffany'

1 9 5 6
'Circus'

1 9 5 7
'Golden Showers'
'White Bouquet'

1 9 5 8
'Fusilier'
'Gold Cup'
'White Knight'

1 9 5 9
'Ivory Fashion'
'Starfire'

1 9 6 0
'Fire King'
'Garden Party'
'Sarabande'

1 9 6 1
'Duet'
'Pink Parfait'

1 9 6 2
'Christian Dior'
'Golden Slippers'
'John S. Armstrong'
'King's Ransom'

1 9 6 3
'Royal Highness'
'Tropicana'

1 9 6 4
'Granada'
'Saratoga'

1 9 6 5
'Camelot'
'Mister Lincoln'

1 9 6 6
'American Heritage'
'Apricot Nectar'
'Matterhorn'

1 9 6 7
'Bewitched'
'Gay Princess'
'Lucky Lady'
'Roman Holiday'

1 9 6 8
'Europeana'
'Miss All-American Beauty'
'Scarlet Knight'

1 9 6 9
'Angel Face'
'Comanche'
'Gene Boerner'
'Pascali'

1 9 7 0
'First Prize'

1 9 7 1
'Aquarius'
'Command Performance'
'Redgold'

1 9 7 2
'Apollo'
'Portrait'

1 9 7 3
'Electron'
'Gypsy'
'Medallion'

1 9 7 4
'Bahia'
'Bon Bon'
'Perfume Delight'

1 9 7 5
'Arizona'
'Oregold'
'Rose Parade'

1 9 7 6
'America'
'Cathedral'
'Seashell'
'Yankee Doodle'

1 9 7 7
'Double Delight'
'First Edition'
'Prominent'

1 9 7 8
'Charisma'
'Color Magic'

1 9 7 9
'Friendship'
'Paradise'
'Sundowner'

1 9 8 0
'Cherish'
'Honor'
'Love'

1 9 8 1
'Bing Crosby'
'Marina'
'White Lightnin''

1 9 8 2
'Brandy'
'French Lace'
'Mon Cheri'
'Shreveport'

1 9 8 3
'Sun Flare'
'Sweet Surrender'

1 9 8 4
'Impatient'
'Intrigue'
'Olympiad'

1 9 8 5
'Showbiz'

1 9 8 6
'Broadway'
'Touch of Class'
'Voodoo'

1 9 8 7
'Bonica'
'New Year'
'Sheer Bliss'

1 9 8 8
'Amber Queen'
'Mikado'
'Prima Donna'

1 9 8 9
'Class Act'
'Debut'
'New Beginning'
'Tournament of Roses'

1 9 9 0
'Pleasure'

1 9 9 1
'Carefree Wonder'
'Perfect Moment'
'Sheer Elegance'
'Shining Hour'

1 9 9 2
'All That Jazz'
'Brigadoon'
'Pride 'n' Joy'

1 9 9 3
'Child's Play'
'Rio Samba'
'Solitude'
'Sweet Inspiration'

1 9 9 4
'Caribbean'
'Midas Touch'
'Secret'

1 9 9 5
'Brass Band'
'Singin' in the Rain'

1 9 9 6
'Carefree Delight'
'Livin' Easy'
'Mt. Hood'
'St. Patrick'

1 9 9 7
'Artistry'
'Scentimental'
'Timeless'

1 9 9 8
'Fame!'
'First Night'
'Opening Light'
'Sunset Celebration'

INDEX